What people are saying about *Parallel Dreams*:

Still life, with crows:
So rich with detail. Tightly written.   ~Zachary Guadamour

Riding the tides of the moon:
This left me breathless, shaken and hopeful... so incredibly
beautiful.   ~ Rebecca Clark Gober

Chapter 2
I descend this bittersweet verse on lines like steps on a
heartfelt ladder.   ~ L Douglas St Ours

Leading with my left foot:
I love the childhood memory sifted through a more mature
perspective.   ~Leigh Spencer

The book of secrets:
One of THE most amazingly beautiful pieces I have read in
a long time. Classic, eternal, graceful, brilliant.
                                         ~Chris Dickerson
Shades of black:
A haunting and bittersweet piece.   ~JoAnn Gaynor

Rose colored glasses:
It's amazing how something beautiful can come from
 a wound.   ~ Sean Tully

White noise:
Wonderful, touching slice of life, very artfully yet distinctly
delivered.   ~David A. Neves

Mandarin orange:
Like soft water color strokes is your imagery here.
                                         ~ Rory Jackson

Parallel dreams:
You wove a magical spell with this.   ~Gail Dormire

Paradise, not lost:
A beautiful blurring of reality in this poem. ~ Peter Doyle

Sanctuary:
Delighted at the ease with which you so comfortably
convey your thoughts.   ~Debra Roberts

High wire:
High wire walking is for the brave of heart. I like how the
inward reflection becomes a discussion of life and its trials.
                                        ~John Sayles

Why:
I adore this. It is so filled with truth and wisdom, and so
beautifully executed.   ~Katherine Wyatt

One…loose…thread:
I've read maybe a hundred thousand poems. I have a
hundred of them that I adore. A few that I cherish. This
poem will be my favorite. It is perfection in every way.
                                    ~Elaine MeaTwosocks

Lead white:
Absolutely brilliant. So full of wonderful imagery and
emotion.   ~ Michael Night

Impermanence:
The emotion here is a warm rush that possesses everything
it touches. You touched me.   ~Dwayne St. Romain

Wow! This is such a balanced piece between the necessities
of everyday realities and the simple beauty that surrounds
during rare peaceful moments. I love the metaphor and
think the last line hammers...well...mortars it home.
                                        ~Leigh Spencer

Parallel Dreams

Poems by

Janet Scott McDaniel

Janet Scott McDaniel

Published by Janet Scott McDaniel

ISBN-10: 1475283113
ISBN-13: 978-1475283112

Printed in the United States of America

The Light and other Collected Poems
Parallel Dreams

Available in softcover, e-book, and Kindle versions:
www.amazon.com
www.barnesandnoble.com

Dedication:

For my husband Odie, who has had to share me with a
laptop filled with words once I began writing again.
None of this would have been possible without his
patience, encouragement, support, and love.

And for my son Greg, for without him pushing me to share
my work with the public at an open mic night, *The Light*
and *Parallel Dreams* may not have come into existence.

My deep love and appreciation to you both…

Acknowledgements

I'd like to express my gratitude to Sean and Tawana Riley, owners of Espresso'n Ice, for supporting the local talent with the open mic nights held at their coffee shop.

Thank you to the many people who have purchased my first book and who follow my writing locally and online. Your enthusiastic support and encouragement keeps me writing.

Many thanks to my daughter Jennifer, a talented photographer, for taking several of the photos used in this book, including the back cover photo.

My thanks to Kelly, a kindred spirit. Your friendship and affirmation of the 'awakening' has changed my life…again.

To my dear friend Chris Dickerson, I give my deepest thanks. You function as my sounding board, and your clarity with regard to my work is invaluable. More importantly, you keep me inspired and motivated. Yes, *I know*, the coach doesn't make the touchdown, but you are one heck of a coach. Much love…

Foreword
by Chris Dickerson

Janet Scott McDaniel and I are a bit like Harper Lee and Truman Capote, except Jan hasn't written *To Kill A Mockingbird* and I'm not a short, flamboyant alcoholic. I also didn't write *Breakfast at Tiffany's* or *In Cold Blood*. But other than those minor points, we're a lot like Harper Lee and Truman Capote, to wit: we've known each other since we were kids, and Jan's one helluva writer.

That she *is* one helluva writer has been obvious since we were kids. Jan was scribbling poetry when we were in high school. That's not unusual; a lot of high school girls write poetry. The difference was, even then, Jan's was *good*.

Some of those poems are contained in her first collection, *The Light and other Collected Poems.* I defy anyone to tell the difference, in terms of quality, from something Jan wrote in the early 1970's to something she composed in 2011.

What's been most remarkable to me has been to watch her journey as a poet since *The Light* was published. The work contained in *The Light* is wonderful, mystical, woven through with the influences of our shared Celtic heritage, beautiful, pristine and haunting.

The poems contained in this current collection "kick it up a notch." The colors are richer, the weave is thicker, the echoes longer. Jan's a true artist, totally incapable of repeating herself, always finding new ways to express her deepest thoughts and clear emotions.

   The Light and *Parallel Dreams* are sterling companion pieces in poetry. While Jan is unique unto herself as a poet, the work in both books continues the tradition of such poets as Dylan Thomas and John Berryman. With them – as with Jan – the music of the language is everything; the music of the language carries the emotional impact.

   There are times when I'm riding along with one of her poems, not entirely sure where the journey is headed although I'm enjoying the trip, then I'll come to the end – and all I can do is sit back and whisper.... "wow."

I trust you will, too…

Chris Dickerson
novelist, playwright and poet
Hollywood, Ca. 2012

Introduction:

I am constantly amazed by this journey that has swept me once again into the world of poetry.

For those of you unfamiliar my work, let me say that you are not alone. I have written poetry all my life, but I have only began writing poetry again, after a 25 year hiatus, in November 2010.

How I got to this point is detailed briefly in my book *The Light and other Collected Poems*, which contains the best of my writings from the past 40 years.

I never intended for work to be made public. My son Greg, much to my chagrin, signed me up for an open mic night at a coffee shop here in town, Espresso 'N Ice. I read my poetry publicly to make him happy, thinking that nothing would come of it. The response was encouraging, so I read at more open mic nights held there.

I re-connected with my high school friend Chris Dickerson - a very talented writer living in Hollywood- in November 2010 after a 33 year separation. Chris became my sounding board and, in the spring of 2011, he told me to think about compiling a book. Book?! That was never on my radar. Suddenly it was in the realm of possibility and that fall I published *The Light.*

The *Parallel Dreams* collection evolved, in style and tone, into something deeper and more profound. Worlds and lives that came before are never totally gone, reminders are all around us. Life experiences can parallel even though the principals are separated by great distances. I live and dream in more than my current world. We all do.

I'd love to be able to tell you that I plan the poems and think them through to create a specific allegory or metaphor, but the truth is that most of the time, when they begin to create themselves in my mind, they begin to pour onto the page often taking a direction that I did not plan. Sometimes the catalyst is a word, or a phrase, a deeply felt emotion, or even an image that I have seen.

I believe my fine art and psychology background manifests itself in my work because I am very attuned to the visual imagery while I am deftly crafting the words to evoke emotion. If I can create within you that sense of joy or despair, reflection or inspiration, or create a new train of thought - that means I have accomplished what I was inspired to do - touch your heart.

The most important part of my journey is that - by writing again, and the sharing of that work publicly- I have come to terms with the realization that you can be different, and that isn't necessarily a bad thing. My writing has led me into the next chapter of my life- my life as a poet.

With this collection I begin the next 40 years. Thank you for joining me on the journey.

Take my hand and
together we'll explore...

Parallel
Dreams

Once in a Blue Moon

I wait beneath a moonlit night
by the twisted tree;
to a nightingale's sad song
we dance… the moon and me.

We move together across the sky
as days and years glide past,
I whisper fervently the same refrain:
will my true love come at last?

Never does he answer me,
a smile plays upon his face;
so I keep my vigil by the twisted tree,
accepting his silence
                    …with grace.

Smoke

Under a deep blue veil
the night air is cool and still.
Stars wink in the heavens;
wind's breath rustles dry leaves.

A shadowy column drifts upward
      ~ smoke ~
curling from a red ember
held in fingers strong with conviction.

Dark whispers a quiet hush
      to blot out the insanity,
letting reality steal a few tortured breaths.

Memories drift in translucent wisps,
their scent lingering as seconds,
    then minutes, pass;
a heavy sigh the only sound.

Thinking… always thinking

Leaning into a light that paled the sun;
painting with watercolors in the rain;
two lives washed to white.

Red ember flares anew,
sending twisting swirls rising into the beyond;

truth carried to the stars;

to be remembered only in darkness
  beneath the silent gaze of the moon.

A Lesson from Mona Lisa

People drift aimlessly about the room like water
circling a drain;

their voices a constant hum, the drone of a swarm of
bees,

never disturbing the solitary figure in the vortex.

Wearing unkempt clothes with slept-in-them wrinkles,

dark shoe-button eyes, stare unblinking from a
hollow-cheeked face;

light brown hair, a tangled mass of knots resisting a
combing by shaking fingers.

A deep breath forces peace deeper into the
bloodstream, life's survival drug,

taking the mind to a place of tranquility - a river with
mountains in the distance.

Sitting up a little straighter, folding hands upon a
lady's finest gown;

corners of the mouth begin to tug at trembling lips,
softening the eyes,

letting a bit of the soul's mystery show through.

Just sitting on the edge of a bed

quietly studying the reflection in a mirror,

trying to remember how to smile.

Mona Lisa by Leonardo da Vinci

Parallel Dreams

Translucent with age
you walk with me,
always remaining on the threshold
of my shadowy memory,
    refusing
to step into the light.

You streak the window to my soul
running down like tears
falling from a silver sky.

I tread in silence
sensing a universe that is oddly calm,
knowing that a careless word
could break the spell.

Here in the darkness of night
when my dreams are still,
with a heart burned to gutter black,
I sit with the ashes;

bending with the winds of time,
as I watch moonlight dance
upon a wine-dark sea.

I look above to the stars
to find you once again,

knowing you will come
and be fearless with me;

knowing your warmth
will melt the early morning frost
on my heart.

So I wait

to steal back the breath
  you stole from me,

when dawn winked upon us
    in colors of pink
                    and gold.

Paradise, not lost

In the twilight of my awakening,
lying motionless, eyes closed;
I am warmed by the sun
as a cool breeze washes over me.

My soul surrenders to the tranquility,
soothed by the sound
of rhythmic ocean waves.
I long to remain in this tropical paradise
as body and mind rest ...heal.

In the way sun burns off morning fog,
reality begins to creep into my reverie,
the momentary disorientation unsettling.
Realization dawns that I cannot stay here
in this, my own private limbo.

As I slowly open my eyes
the final pieces shift into place…

setting sun creeping across the floor
  toward the bed where my little girl sleeps.

I lift my head off the arm of the chair,
blanket falling from my shoulders as I stand
smiling at the innocence I see upon her face.
The sound machine is her favorite gift from me
for she loves to sleep to the music of ocean waves.

I tiptoe quietly from the room,
peace settling upon my heart as gently
      as the snow falling outside her window.

The Book of Secrets

My fingers trace faintly embossed lines
that grace the ancient leather cover.

Within its well-worn pages
there lies a wisp of almost;
words flying on gossamer wings
in the twilight between knowing
and not knowing.

My visions dance to music from the black keys,
floating upon the page in fiery luminescence,
yet they have no more permanence
than breath upon a mirror.

Ink pales upon the page as I read on
        finding no final chapter
yet wanting, needing there to be one.

Only a fierce knowing remains
as within the echoes of lifetimes
we find each other once again
        together upon a page.

Dare I succumb to eternal longing?

Intoxicated by the fragrance of possibilities
I dream of you in celestial starlight;
my night shadows receding
as goodbye becomes a second chance,
the warmth of a golden dawn.

Pen in hand,
black is the color of my words as
I etch the final chapter onto vellum stone.

Gently closing the book,
I hold it tight

    breathing deeply of the past
    exhaling the present

as I hold you

saying the words
                I dare not speak.

Impermanence

I am a mason,
for survival's sake.

Brick by brick
with mortar I build ~
to keep in,
to keep out,
all that would tear at my heart,
all that would make me

ache

long

wish

remember

I stay focused,
with busy hands
building each new day
strong and solid,
full of kindness,
love,
and laughter.

Until

the sapphire night
blankets my world,
quieting my mind,
settling my heart.

As I wander
alone,
it's then that I hear
the scrape of stone
against stone,
a low rumble
as my walls

slowly

fall

and I must embrace
the truth of my life
once again.

Indigo fades to blush pink,
and in the warmth of the
rising sun,

 I pick up my trowel.

White Noise

I struggle to read
your indistinct pencil lines
whispered upon the page

while you hold fast
to a sheet filled to over-flowing
with my bold black strokes.

I look up,
glasses perched on my nose
brow creased in concentration,
to see your smiling face
and I smile back;
an automaton
mimicking your actions.

You speak your love in subtlety,
while I spray paint our names
on the water tower.

And so I squint,
and tilt the page
trying once again
to make out the words
that I know are there

wanting them to be as bold
as the memory from my childhood
when my father
stamped the letters of my name
into the newly fallen snow.

Riding the Tides of the Moon

I traveled in life's spring
  upon an overgrown path,
pockets full of crumbled hopes
as shadows of the world
  surrounded me in starlit velvet.
Dawn seemed forever lost
   as I rode the tides of the moon.

Under a crescent moon,
from muted periphery
   your dark eyes emerged,
daring me with danger.
Standing at the crossroads of time,
  we basked in the light,
the awakening deep within our souls
 …the old ways
         calling us home.

Though I could not see,
   I believed
 in the granting of solace to kindred hearts.
I offered you starlight on my fingertips,
in my cupped hands
  molten light from a brilliant moon.
With whispers
   I captured an angel
for in the light of the stars,
   your eyes glowing dark within blue,
     you showed me your love.

Lives transition and transform,
  forever bending in time's gentle wind.
I have tilled sorrows and planted tears.
I have stood on shifting sands of promises,

longing for sure footing of stone.
I watched sand flow in the hourglass
until in lantern's flickering light
        shadows of dreams re-appeared,
    for at long last you are here.

No longer am I a glassy countenance
    in the dark side of a mirror.
Just as a bird in a cage
    spreads its wings to fly,
before you I stand in welcome,
    rapier brandished high,
the song of the old ways
        thundering within my chest.

Take me with you on this journey
    upon the never-ending road of cascading stones;
riding until the moon meets the sea
    as we cast aside the velvet shroud of darkness.
For in cathedrals of the forest
    will we find the answers,
        ask the questions.

We will cross the bridge with lessons learned
when the barriers of time turn to dust.

No longer do we live
    only within almost-forgotten dreams.
To our kingdom which lies beyond the stars
    are we destined to journey
                together
                    ...riding the tides of the moon.

One. . . Loose . . .Thread. . .

I see you unraveling.
I am powerless to stop it.

A few stolen moments cannot erase days
filled with uncertainty as
        your life spins out of control.

I watch you scrabbling,
grabbing with both hands
to try to stop the madness,
to try to create a sane world;

so I hold you tighter, but nothing changes.

You are unraveling

with a smile upon your face,
appearing strong to the world.

But I see the truth in your eyes
as your body moves in brutal honesty,
    always unfulfilled.

I envelope you in my love
and it is not enough,
could never *be* enough,
                to heal you.

You lower your sorrow-filled eyes
and I follow your gaze
to the hem of my soul,
            and I see
                    one... loose... thread . . .

Sanctuary

In peaceful slumber, I drift
as shadows cross the moon.
A thief, silent in the night,
the words tiptoe into my dreams
stealing my security;
demons dancing on fire;
an assassin's bullet.

Is it just an owl's cry
that flies soft upon the night wind?
Or a coyote's howl
transforming into a low gibbering moan
wailing the agonies of the damned?
Realization comes with the dawn
    ...it is my own.

From room to room
silence echoes as I softly tread
into darker nights of the soul;
memories becoming elusive shadows;
visions fading to whispers in misty eyes.

At the window I stand
with morning sun upon my face,
warming me with promise.
I feel the distant drumbeats,
my heart beating within my chest.
I raise my eyes as with a rush of wings,
birds take to flight
and I see
        ......the sky did not fall.

Leading with my Left Foot

I close my eyes as I dance with my father,
my feet on his shoes.
He holds me close swinging me around
a rag doll, looking up
to watch the world spin above me.

On the whirling dervish, years pass in an eye blink.
Day spins into night, dark into light;
the everyday world a kaleidoscope of colors
flashing before my eyes
as the minutiae that swallows
every minute of every day… swallows me.

I will never be Houdini,
will never escape the chains,
destined to be swept away…

my fingers only ever brushing the fringe of calm,
the perception of normalcy,
as minutes blur into the forever.

But undaunted,
        I reach out
                one more time.

Epiphany

Not by my choosing
I am bound by a gossamer thread,
to be drawn ever closer
as light and shadow shift around me.

Never did I dream
I could feel the ticking of the clock,
or see that of which I know not;
sensing what is no longer here to be sensed,
as with trembling fingers
I touch the hem of the other world.

Not by my choosing
I have watched magic take wing;
seen proof that my world will not shatter
into shards as bright as glass.

Not by my choosing
but with humble gratitude for their signs
which bring me to my knees,

my tears glistening
as they fall to the floor.

For now there is no doubt,
if indeed there ever was.

Not by my choosing did this begin,
but by my choice will it remain.

Forever will I listen
to the breeze that whispers
among the leaves.

She Talks to Rain in the Moonlight

They call her crazy,
    but I think her name is Rose.

Solitary in the woods, her house sits,
  weathered wood and gingerbread,
rusted iron gate and forget-me-nots.

I hear she wanders,
rose pink ribbons in her hair,
singing songs to birds in the wood,
soprano notes floating upon the wind

telling
    of dreams that set her heart on fire,
    of reasons she takes another step
      on this tortured path called life;

telling
the un-countable little things
    which aren't little at all.

I hear she tucks in the flowers at night
nestles them under evening fog;
with evenstar as her guide
  she talks to rain in the moonlight.

Madness wears many disguises.

The moon is full,
  so I step outside

      … to talk to the rain.

Maybe \\'mā-bē/   adv. / n.

Strange is the power
of five little letters.

Maybe!

I am buoyed
to joy beyond description
by the possibility of fulfillment;
    of dreams to be realized;
    of hope nurtured to fruition.
I am filled to over-flowing
with only a tentative promise
dangling before my heart.

Maybe.

Suddenly blinded,
I close my eyes,
falling off the cliff
into the depths below.
The shock of the coldness
crushes the air from my lungs,
and as I drift deeper,
watching the shimmering light
fade farther away
I wonder if it is worth the effort
    to fight for the surface;
    to face my life again.

Maybe. . .

Lesson Learned

Within, without, above, below,
time does not stop, it does not slow;
heartless, cruel, we call it then.
Time - rarely do we call it friend

To thief of youth, of precious years
we bequeath a river of bitter tears;
moaning anguish of dreams lost,
shadows shimmering in winter's frost.

Balm to heal wounds to the heart,
fading pain when loved ones depart;
only its passage then can mend,
we become a willow, learn how to bend.

Learn to become a keeper of fire,
of passion, of living life's desire;
until reaching the veil at journey's end
reluctantly, time becomes our friend.

Time does not stop, forever will it flow,
a lesson learned in soft candlelight glow.

Penny Arcade

Penny clinks into the slot,
hesitant hand turns the crank.
Flickering images
in shades of gray
begin to move;
life in motion.

No sound,
just familiar faces,
places,
times that tugged at the heart.

The good,
the bad,
the ones not worth mentioning
or almost forgotten,
flickering past.

Life,
moving as fast
or as slow,
as the hand that turns the crank
allows.

Only here
is there control
over what we see,
what we feel;
here we choose
our moment in time.

Rewind...?
it's only possible
at the movies.

Walking the Ghost Road

Tears of dew
fall upon the path of sacred stone
where moccasin-clad feet
shuffle,leather upon stone,
as drums beat low
  upon the night wind.

Softly,
kindred spirits chant,
dark eyes within painted faces;
bodies circling the sacred fire,
in harmony with the hypnotic rhythm
of the shell shakers;

feathers and beads
speaking of a history
as ancient as Mother Earth.

In eternal cadence they move as one,
their voices a graceful hymn:

     of lessons told,
     history shared;

tributes honoring those
who have walked beyond the stars.

For only in the knowledge of the ancients,
can we ever hope to find
our place
  upon the ghost road.

The Callanish Stones

upon the isle
standing stones
high above the sea

pilgrims trek
hesitant touch
drawn by energy

midsummer sunrise
by cuckoo's herald
the 'shining one' you'll see

avenue points to
midsummer moon setting
beyond Clisham mountain

theories abound
worship
astronomy

eternal silence
weathered gazes
ancient history

unspoken truth
profound peace
timeless mystery

The Callanish Stones are situated near the village of
Callanish on the west coast of Lewis in the Outer Hebrides
(Western Isles of Scotland)

Construction of the site took place between 2900 and 2600 BC. The 13 primary stones form a circle about 13m in diameter, with a long approach avenue of stones to the north, and shorter stone rows to the east, south, and west. The overall layout of the monument recalls a distorted Celtic cross. The individual stones vary from around 1m to 5m in height.

It has been speculated, among other theories, that the stones form a calendar system based on the position of the moon. Professor Alexander Thom suggested that the alignment of the stone avenue (when looking southward) pointed to the setting of midsummer full moon behind a distant mountain called Clisham.

Local tradition says that giants who lived on the island refused to be converted to Christianity by Saint Kieran and were turned into stone as a punishment. Another local belief says that at sunrise on midsummer morning, the "shining one" walked along the stone avenue, "his arrival heralded by the cuckoo's call." This legend could be a folk memory recalling the astronomical significance of the stones.

As Soft Winds Shake the Barley

He saw her first in morning mist
As barefoot upon the cobbles,
With copper curls bound in a twist
She ran, hands full of baubles
To see sun warm upon his face
The morning she met early
And so she ran with child-like grace
As soft winds shook the barley

In strong arms he drew her tight
And spun her in sun's rays
In green eyes there shone a light
That lanced the misty haze
'Twas bliss two hearts in summer wind
Woe to he who'd hurt her dearly
As from his lips the words spilled then
As soft winds shook the barley

Died the laughter in the glen
Remorse his answer to her "why?"
Trinkets spilled into the wind,
From her lips a mournful cry
Tho' sad he kissed away her tears
His love he would show clearly
With gold he promised her his years
While soft winds shook the barley.

Alone she wanders in valley green
Adorned in life's fall colors
Blood vengeance, she feels it keen
In death he lies among his 'brothers'
Gold held true a promise made
Love strong and true found rarely
And still soft winds blow down the glade
and shake the golden barley.

To Wander in Moonshadow

Absentmindedly,
my fingers seek out the stone that hangs
from the black silk cord around my neck.
It absorbs my warmth
   as I gently stroke its surface,
my mind drifting like clouds across the sky.

All that I am
   lies entombed for eternity
within honey colored amber.

My façade crumbled
and I faced you in reality,
two shadows dancing to the nightsong
that only kindred hearts can hear,

surrendering to our smoldering fire;

the moon's reflection luminous in your eyes,
as through a starlit sky
   I fall upon clouds of white;

an angel's lips upon my brow.

Deep within my dreams
      you live,
your warmth still here
   resting upon my heart.

You are with me as I wander
in a singing night wind,
while into my hands
                  the mists weep.

My angel in black fur, Coal.

Angels in Black Fur

It's a mild day, for December;
a few brown leaves still lie upon the ground.
Dark and overcast, for two days now rain has fallen,
tapping out its message on the roof;
tricking the clematis on the mailbox
into blooming one last time.

Raindrops, are they angel's tears that fall?
Symbolic in so many ways, yet, here… now…
as I watch them dance upon the driveway
they are reassurance, and hope.

Angel touches, warm and insistent
clamber about my feet,
one still with a newborn's squeak;
devotion ~ total and pure,
my angels in black fur.

I gather them to me, hold them close;
good luck to the Celts,
shunned by superstitious society;
purrs of adoration, my white noise,
blotting out this crazy mixed-up world.

I'll find them, of that I'm sure;
the brave hearts
willing to go against the perception;
forever homes
that will receive life's greatest blessing.

Rain falls
and I smile, for I am smothered
in unconditional love
        from angels in black fur.

High Wire

Upon the wooden platform I stand
contemplating my moment of truth,
summoning courage,
my heart beating wildly within my chest.

I can do this.

I place one foot upon the wire,
gently shifting my weight,
finding my balance.

Step by tentative step
I begin to walk;
steel cable taut under my feet,
disappearing into the distance.

Slow and steady I move,
with carefully regulated breaths,
hands lightly holding the balancing pole.
I feel the subtle shifts,
make corrections,
feeling the tenuous hold on life
through my shoe's thin leather soles.

I can do this.
I *will* do this.
I take a deep breath,
willing my soul to be calm,
repeating the mantra: *don't look down.*

You can only be afraid
            if you acknowledge the risk.

I fix my eyes securely upon the future,
a smile beginning to play at the corners of my lips.

I make progress one foot after the other;
eyes turning steely with new-found strength,
their sight never wavering from the goal.

I am doing this…

Corrective shifts come naturally now;
my confident steps becoming faster
as the platform signaling
the end of my journey approaches.
My world changes forever,
and all I can breathe is joy
        as my toe touches wood.

© Getty Images

Still Life, with Crows

Held by a frame of faded gold,
weak winter sun shines
through twisted oak branches,
the hill upon which they stand
    falling away to mist.

Above the trees
    inky black
against steel gray clouds that fill the sky
a murder of crows fly,
            wings outspread,
                    slowly circling.

Encased in splintered wood,
through a cracked windowpane
pale yellow rays tiptoe silently
across the dusty floor,
    past the scent of cobwebs
    and rumpled sheets,
to lie with whispers
left upon the pillow.

It hangs askew,
paint cracking and peeling
    on the aged canvas
as seasons pass without sound;
yet, when the wind follows free

in the whispers left behind,
deep secret wisdom remains,
    in their echoes
 still inky black upon a steel gray sky,
        crows
                still fly.

The Loneliest Number

Looking through the kitchen window
I can almost hear the wind
through the sun-dappled grass,

trees laughing
    in colors of red
        and gold.

I see it fall

one leaf of brilliant red
caught by the breeze
as it says goodbye
        to home.

Carried away from me
it journeys past exotic lights
and ancient grounds,

sailing along
    to where the wind fancies.

Into the stream it tumbles,
a flash of vermilion
amid sunsparkles on the water;

floating along,

swirling in the eddies,

    sometimes

snagging on the shoreline,

before being swept away
by the callous hand
          of the current;

destined
to drift alone
in the rumored hush
               of moonlight;

endlessly searching
for echoes of warmth
said to lie
          just around the bend.

Highway 13

Some journeys
don't require a map.

It's not my first time
down this road;

the detour happening
without warning…

again.

Signposts are still there,
weathered,
sometimes invisible.

The road is still rough,
difficult to navigate,

yet,

the journey is familiar;
tho' faces and places
change with the seasons.

Traveling alone-
that decision made for me,
leaving too much time to think,

sensations becoming cumulative
because
        the heart remembers.

Darkness slowly closes in,
making it hard to see the road.

I look up
     and sigh.

I remember now…

just storm clouds
passing overhead,
bringing a rain
of hell's fire
to be endured
once more.

And I will.

I always do.

Magic Happened

Magic happened when you opened the door,
        the years fell away;
a younger woman floated across the floor.

You said with a smile, "First things first."

With a burning intensity
        you pulled me close
            …I still held my purse.

I breathed you in - a hypnotic drug;
        the world disappeared;
I longed to remain in your arms,
        lost in your hug.

We sat down to talk, but it was still there
among our clasped hands, warm and tender:

    ~desire ~

        suspended in the air.

and I remembered….

"I love to talk to you.
                I love to hold you more."

I reached for you, pulled your body to mine.
We melted together, you and I;
there I could have stayed, for all time.

drifting in your arms

left breathless

by your lips upon mine

begging time to stop

memorizing the taste of your lips

the feel of your heart beating against mine

~ then you whisper ~

"I want to take you upstairs

and make love to you

for hours

....days

...weeks."

I feel the world drop from under my feet.

I will remember this moment,

your lips igniting a fire within.

I know that I will never get enough,

because
....magic happened.

Gypsy

In the great hall, music flows;
brushing across rough stone walls,
snuggling in dark velvet drapes.

In iron sconces, candles flicker,
    shadows of dreams
dancing upon he who sits
among tables adorned with silver
  and gold.

Dressed in ribbons,
through the stone arch she appears,
    gently swaying;
swan-like hands telling a story
as his dark eyes draw her nearer.

Upon her lips
  a shy smile plays,
emerald green eyes flash mischief
as slender fingers pull a jeweled pin;
auburn curls tumble with their release.

Fighting the yearning no longer
  he reaches for her...
she twirls just beyond his reach;
across his outstretched hand
drift ribbons of blue
  and gold.

The music fades;
    one by one,
candle flames transform into smoke.

In the far corner of the room,
his head bows;

within a scarred face,
darkened eyes slowly close
to etch the memory.

He rises
setting a dented pewter cup
upon the battered wood table;

melting into the shadows of the night,

carrying in his heart
the echoes of her laughter.

There's a little black spot on the sun today

Yeah, I know…
I'm humming it too.

Decidedly discombobulated
while everything is in flux fashizzle
as I ponder the current curfuffle.

A ridiculous blathering brouhaha!

Sometimes…

all I really want
is just a little schadenfreude.

Would that really be so bad?

I know what you're thinking,
but you see
I'm not just egg nog,
I've gone a little nutmeg.

The truth is
I'll feel a whole lot better
after a big spoonful of
milk of amnesia.

Astronomy 101

gravitational pull
gently felt
before the needle
ticked on the meter
subtle shift in energy
attention
light

new planet hypothesis
proven
by gradual decline
of words upon the page
infrequent hellos
distance
of body
mind
heart

universe expanding
one declines
another grows
it always will
being kinetic
not static

life exists on more
than just one planet
that's the theory,
   anyway

to that end
I love you
enough
to let go

Rose Colored Glasses

porch creaks from measured steps
rain drips in steady cadence
heart now beats a broken rhythm

clarity a sudden thunderbolt
innocent comment striking
the soft part of my soul

unexpected

unprepared

ignorance was bliss
until you let me in on the secret
closing the door
pinching my heart
until it bled

her shadow eclipses my eyes
tears stream in rivulets
maintaining decorum
the phone, my mask

magic evaporates
sudden intake of breath
comprehension
of another ending
dawning

I am the gazelle
in the jaws of the lion:
limp
accepting
resigned

letting go requires courage

and I remember...
    you can't lose
        what you never had.

The Guide

A rising sun peeks above the horizon,
reaching out
to gently run its fingers across
buds and blooms growing
along a path paved in alabaster
    and mercury.

Short is the journey, yet
in abundance does poesy flourish,
sun's warmth coaxing growth,
its gentle rays fluent
   in starlight
      and goofy.

Rising steadily to lead the way,
fighting bravely a stroke of fate
to climb sierra trails.

Spinning magic in curling waves
that crash thunder upon the shore,
before receding
in a humble reticence,
   to glow softly in brandy
   swirling slowly in a glass.

Slipping below the horizon,
day's journey drawing to an end,
      yet
in a constancy born
  of fierce determination,
will it rise again to find poesies
waiting
   to bloom in its light.

Blue

In a new dawn
indigo recedes into steel.

Floating slowly toward a mist of powder,
swirls of baby and light
            converge

fading   to simply

        sky.

Breathing in warmth under a denim canopy
while draped in prussian and cobalt.

Walking endless fields in summer's electric,
hands overflowing with periwinkle
            and cornflower.

Joyously skirting the perimeter of cerulean
            hesitantly
dipping toes into turquoise,

        longing
to experience distant ultramarine.

Royal courses through veins,
that elusive power of midnight
            as navy transforms to dark

leaving behind
        only fleeting visions
                of gun-metal
                        and sapphire.

Deep Purple

Lost again,
mind drifting,
snuggling deep
  within soft sheets of mulberry,
trying to summon the forgiveness of violets-

the scent that remains upon the heel that crushed it.

I share her love of violets.

Searching for new footing
in this upside down world,

        when a parent
        becomes the child once again.

Wielding sword against mauve untruths,
bloody finger pricks from thistles;

soft cries of wisteria on the night wind.

Orchids still bloom on the windowsill,
   a gift to honor deep purple pain.

        white streaked with fuschia

        my soul streaked with plum

Just breathe…

breathe deeply of the lilacs
that grew outside her window
           years ago.

Breathe the lavender
   she picked from the field
      to calm my mind;

…all the while
   absently turning
        round and round,

her ring of amethyst
   I still wear upon my finger.

Shades of Black

Night sky whispers its greeting,
the muted caws of crows that sit
upon the house's broken gingerbread

     waiting

          I see dark.

Through silver ribbons of moonlight
a raven flies, circling slowly,
its wise black eyes watching the shadowy figure
distorted by a broken glass windowpane,

     slowly walking,

bare feet leaving silent footprints
through soot lying upon cold ebony floors.

          You can't see dark.

Fingers trace the length of jet beads
held by a small gold clasp, centuries old.

     A lover's eye

captured in watercolor upon ivory,
coal black hair and a single gray eye,
finely painted, it lies under glass.

          I see lighter shades
                of dark.

A lover's tryst

captured not in ink upon the page,
nor breathless passion of intertwined bodies

but with a brush with a single hair.

Often proudly worn - this secret devotion;
eye's identity known only to the wearer.

A love story - now lost to the ages

yet words are over-rated
                        and unnecessary

when you gaze
                into the window to the soul.

Mandarin Orange

Cherry trees were blooming
when she first walked down the lane,
pink blossom rain falling at her feet.

Familiarity warmed her hesitant smile
as I invited her to come sit beside me
on my concrete porch steps,
    grateful
for the distraction in my thinking.

I offered her a wedge of my tangerine
but instead, she touched
my sleeve of burnt sienna suede

    to get my attention.

My dark eyes drifted to hers,
locking at last on soft green.
Through the years
I had looked before,
    but never truly seen.

    I saw now

a rose just beginning to bloom;
a promise of sunrise dawning
   bright and warm

    unspoken questions

    unspoken love

But for me there existed only a noir world,
my journey a solitary one;
a vagabond offering only sunset

  unspoken answers

  unspoken love.

In autumn, when sunlight faded
upon hay bales and pumpkins in the field,

I walked the lane one last time

  to wave a bittersweet goodbye
  to a green-eyed beauty

in a dress of mandarin orange.

Hunter Green

Footsteps in stealth upon moss and fern
plunging deep into pine forest shadows,
gently brushing past sage and mint;
the fragrance of eucalyptus
a thick celadon veil hanging in the air.

Eyes flashing emerald anger;
the communion of souls
remain visions suspended in clouds of chartreuse.

Talismans of jade held in white-knuckled fists;
the taste of lime
          tart upon the tongue.

Embodying judge and jury,
convicting in absentia
among twisted trunks of olive trees.

Arms outspread,
spewing forth to the heavens
the verdict in kelly green;

a black hole of darkness
    snapping at the heels
threatening to devour into lifelessness.

A verdict given in marble halls
with towering malachite columns
is still not vindication.
Punishment does not rescind pain.

Journey on into the night

   footsteps silent upon moss and fern,
   brushing gently past sage and mint

to wander deep into pine forest shadows.

Breathe deeply

   the fragrance of eucalyptus
   that still hangs in the air

like a thick celadon veil.

Lead White

Ants within an anthill,
patrons drift about the Hague,
wandering past a small painting
        simplistic
a young girl in a blue and yellow turban,
a pearl earring.

        Listen…
for within her eyes lie the echoes.

Leather shoes with silver buckles
        slap against wooden steps
        leading to the second floor.
Impatient hands fling open large windows;
flat north light floods the room.

Ivory linen, stretched tight on a frame
sits upon an easel.
From the mind's eye, a ghost appears,
created in rich colors, carefully placed.

With a deft hand
        like a magician conjuring magic
        with smoke and mirrors
attention turns back to the canvas
the focus now upon details.

A quick dab of paint,
        a flick of the brush-
a twinkle appears in her eyes,
lips become moist, ready to speak,
window's light reflects in the pearl.

80

A master who creates light
in the darkness.

A simple lesson,
yet through the centuries,
one so many have failed to learn.

I step into the falling snow
but I am snowblind no longer.

Dipping the tip of a brush into paint
I approach the canvas of my life,

ready to create magic

with touches of lead white.

Johannes Vermeer
Girl with a pearl earring
c. 1665- 1667

Primary Red

Persimmon breaks a Spanish dawn,

carnelian spilling across Sevilla's cobbles.

In narrow streets, stone walls echo footsteps,

fiercely proud strides within a suit of lights.

In an arena filled to overflowing

bugle sounds announce corrida.

Crowd roars cheers in cinnabar voices,

demanding vermilion satisfaction.

Matador stands stoic, dark eyes hooded in claret;

a swirling capote flashes magenta and gold,

with lance the dance begins.

Wild cerise eyes charge the danger;

maroon thunders in pounding hooves

consumed by primitive scarlet rage.

Destinies meet, pass after pass,

locked in choreographed burgundy battle;

pulse weakened at last by barbed banderillas.

Ancient blood sport ends as it must-

drawn close by ruby muleta,

a final thrust of flashing steel.

Death steals any pardon

from a bull streaked in Andalusian crimson.

Yellow Fire

Sun burns ochre

    heat

knifing through a butter sky
relentlessly beating

upon bodies rhythmically rocking
upon laden camels plodding
upon dune after cresting dune
upon endless blistering desert.

    Wandering

the quest for caravanserai
shimmering in memories lost.

Splashing in sunshine sparkled rivers,
buttercups held under a youthful chin.
Goldenrod waving a brassy greeting;
as jonquil meadows herald spring.

Scent of lemons heavy in the air
on mountains with ancient stone temples.

Caged under a pale yellow light
deep in a mine shaft's darkness
 the canary sings its lullaby.

Sun burns ochre
searing bitter truth
into those who wander
but are not
        lost.

Hindsight

If I had only known

that the joy of Dad teaching me that card trick before I left for school

that watching my friend's intense dark eyes flash as we talked about writing for hours, his feet propped on the edge of his desk, smoke curling from a cigarette

that hearing a sudden "I love you" from my high school crush during a conversation on the telephone

that seeing Dad for that brief half-hour visit in the hospital after he was admitted

that looking into green eyes as I brushed the hair from Mom's forehead as she lay in bed, saying to me "you're so pretty"

If I had only known
when I walked out your door on a winter's day

that kissing you......

causing my body to remember,

      and my mind to forget,

          ...... would be the last time.

Pendulum

I feel the ticking of the clock,
    the light touch of its fingers;

the passage of time
    silken against my skin.

I close my eyes,
        swaying

the minutes' whisper
          hypnotic

so easy to forget
        where I am in my life

drifting back
      and forth

between fire
    and ice

content
    distracted

until,
  like a father,

moments take my hand
      to guide me
        forward.

Roulette

Tenuous
our hold on life;
never knowing
if our next breath
will be our last
by circumstance,
   or design.

How is change wrought
   from stone
         ...to shifting sand?

We watched them
   fall from the towers;
ten seconds,
   a very public death.

How do you move
beyond pain that eclipses
   rational thought?

She found him,
life taken by choice,
   a private death.

What makes one person slip,
yet another
            ...fall?
Callous disregard for life,

media fodder.
Infirmities, accidents
snuffing lives
of the old,
and the young.

No distinction
between rich or poor,
color or creed.

Our tenuous hold
      the only sure thing
      as we move through life

watching
      the roulette wheel spin,

waiting
      for the ball to drop.

Drifting

Each day you drift farther away,
Once lover you're now just a friend,
For myriad reasons, you could not stay.

Your smile was the light in my day,
I lived for those now and thens.
Each day you drift farther away.

Through sun and storm, in love we played.
I'm often lost in 'remember whens'.
For myriad reasons, you could not stay.

In dreams, my knight the dragon will slay,
But in morning, by myself I defend.
Each day you drift farther away.

In spite of our love, life got in the way,
Together forever, we can only pretend.
For myriad reasons, you could not stay.

My heart you took when you went away;
Seems all good things must come to an end.
Each day you drift farther away.
For myriad reasons, you could not stay.

Why

In a crackling fire the last ember winks out.
Another petal falls from the rose.
The wave crashes, washes back out to sea
leaving cool sand under bare toes.

String slips from tentative fingers,
red balloon floats high out of sight.
A butterfly trapped in a spider's web
stops struggling with all its might.

From a deep wound can come beauty.
One last snowflake drifts down from the sky.
Love's melody suddenly played out of tune.
There are no answers to some questions of why.

Parsimony

There are those who
believe in providence,
destiny, and fate.

Those who charge into life,
Those who choose to wait.

Romantics envision a
fairy-tale ending, with
candlelight and rose petals.

Realists proving life black
and white; no wiggle room
for when the dust settles.

Shaving with Occam's razor,
slicing away the assumptions,
finding truth in the simplest solution
requires no special gumption.

And so with parsimony, that
revered economy of explanation,
the proof of the hypothesis
is the following declaration:

it is what it is.

In the Blink of an Eye

Motorcycle rumbles fade to silence;
the setting sun shining
on the line of abandoned sentinels.

Suits and ties join
leather jackets and chaps
passing through the door.

Shadows fill empty hearts;
minds struggle to find an answer,
each face wearing the same mask,
of disbelief and sorrow.

Sharing stories of friendship,
    a mechanic's talent
    practical jokes,
laughter and applause
mixing with choked words;
diversity finding unity
in sharing unexpected loss.

In silence,
humanity flows from the building;
under a full moon
throaty engines roar to life,
hesitantly leaving
  one
      by one.

Tomorrow,
they will awaken changed,
to ride a different road
under the same sun.

186 Degrees

The phone rings,
and I find myself
trapped
within a glistening web.

Words of spun sugar
creating a sparkling illusion,
so deceptively sweet,
drawing me in.

Their warmth
melting all reservations,
tempting a fall.

Finally unencumbered
by the struggling to achieve
the unattainable,

a sprite I have never met
 - the real me -
begins to breathe.

Dazzled by
    I love you,
    I want you

…pure magic woven
        from sugar glass.

In a sudden rush,
I miss you
tumbles from your lips

...yet not enough
to voice concern,

or to let me rest easy
in your peace;

not enough

to banish my darkness
with your light.

Sugar doesn't melt,
         it decomposes.

It was just a web
  of candy glass

breaking with goodbye

and the brittle click

                of silence.

Conundrum

Night and day,
black and white;
what you say,
and what you do.

You are so convincing
and I want so much
    to believe.
You tell me it is sunlight,
but around me, all is darkness;
I should be warm,
but I feel the cold.

You tell me you love me,
then act like I don't matter;
you say you need me,
then dismiss me.

I am a yo-yo that is
played upon your fingers;
pulled close,
then pushed away.

How am I to know
which is the truth?

Chapter 2

left open
heart's door
shared my life
but nevermore

cruel words
snide remarks
led my soul
into the dark

truth cuts deep
no desire to see
or hear what
becomes of me

lonely world
caustic time
bitter pills
choice is mine

walk away
leave the pain
wash my tears
in the rain

spirit lifts
decision made
chapter ends
I turn the page

Reflection

In silence I walk the shoreline,
waves kissing my feet,
their rhythmic music
    numbing my mind.

On the infinite ocean
my mind sails to the far reaches
searching for understanding,

yet finding that explanations
    explain nothing.

Sand, cool under my feet,
so certain it is firm ground, yet

    with the next kiss upon my feet
    it slips so easily from beneath me,

leaving a momentary struggle
    to regain balance.

Setting sun dips low in the sky
pouring liquid colors of Monet
    upon the water.

With a breathless ache
I etch the moment to heart,
to join the memories
    that keep it beating.

The ocean whispers to the moon.

Tears like pearls lie upon my cheek.

With the darkness, a stillness comes;

an illusion of peace
        in starlight and moon glow.

Silently I continue on,
one foot in front of the other,

smothered in the kisses
                of the waves.

Little Red Moon

Ghostly exhalations
    waft from below,

the chill of the unknown
shivering across the soul.

Trembling hands
light tallow candles,
their feeble light shining
as shadows block the sun.

Little red moon …

walk the twisting path
as stars collide
      in a black sky;

the blood of night,
a fire keeper's water for the soul,
  spilling on flora and fauna;
  spilling on those labeled

    'different'

who cry out in eternal ache-
the beauty and the tragedy being

    ignorance

of the majesty of the difference.

Something old and good and wise
    lies deep within,

waiting
to comb landscapes for lost dreams

waiting
to craft words into wings

waiting
for magic to take flight.

Drink deeply in quiet contemplation-
the blood of night.

Candles wink out,
conceding to a realization
that begins to glow brighter,
that begins to spread warmth,

that begins

...to banish the darkness.

Fine Tuning

White clouds sail across the blue sky,
as a brilliant sun warms my skin;

to the caress of the breeze I succumb,
    closing my eyes…

The signal is strong,
humming in the core of my being;

    a blend of

high voltage wire,
    vibration from a passing train,
        butterfly stomach,
            stage fright.

A never-ending frequency
changing minute by minute,

  igniting nerve endings
into a heightened sense of awareness;
hinting of degrees of a deeper knowing

waiting to be
                discovered
                    acknowledged
                        embraced
                            activated.

It is just beyond
                    seeing,
                        hearing,
                            feeling

yet with each breath the power
sets every cell buzzing, until
I am intoxicated by the transition.

Illumination comes
    with just a little fine tuning,
distortion snapping into sharp focus.

Swaddled in a cocoon no longer,
my soul expands and transforms.

I open my eyes
gazing in wonder at my open hand…

    expecting to see fire

        shooting from my fingertips.

            Can you feel it?

Folded

In the warmth of the light,
fingers interlaced,
we journey-
   two candles
   burning a single flame;
   one voice;

your name resting upon my lips
as I float with you.

A dark misty fog, drifting;
    silence
 slowly folds me into its arms.
Invisible steel bands,
      cold,
   suffocating,
pull me into the vacuum.

Desperately I squirm;
thrashing against that
which swallows me whole;

a modern day Jonah,
  within a whale

  of silence.

Whispers in the night,
  laughter,
    tandem hearts beating …

  all the sounds of you…

        slowly fade away…

The space between breaths

Rain falls
  on my dark September morning;

with the lightning
there comes the briefest flash;
  Alma, decades past;
  a snapshot memory

of an April barely dawning.

Bubbly, never timid;
infectious smile playing upon her lips.

A wide-eyed waif framed in brown hair,
  defining good,
  embodying innocent.

Her questioning hazel eyes

    now yellowed,

she lies watching,

    trusting

in him charged to heal.

The news -
        a thunderbolt in a clear sky.

    unnecessary
    unimaginable
    unbearable

The tender fingers of a child
      gently release their hold.

Floating away
    she whispers…

        … *first, do no harm…*

Still the rain falls …
washing the air to pure,

    unspoiled;

fleeting reflections
of two lives just beginning;

rain transporting me
to another bittersweet place,
      …to Sandy.

Thunderclap - an echo of joyous hands;
    spontaneous laughter,
    bright eyes, ready smile;
a friend to this lonely outcast.

Dark wavy hair she wraps around
  her head at night to straighten.

Peaceful slumber in December's cold
        only an illusion,
a precursor to nightmare.

In pain, she cries out in the night;
gently cradled in her mother's arms
      she floats away…

My world blurs,
a mist drifting before my eyes,
  seen, yet unseen.

In the space between breaths,

  the faintest brush
    of her lips against my cheek;

an acknowledgement

          of remembrance.

In loving memory of my friends:
Alma Wood, age 14, April 1970, and

Sandy Wolfel, age 15, December 1970

In my cherished memories your sweet souls live on...still.

To Touch the Snow on Kilimanjaro

Driven like a madman
I climb higher,
fingers scrabbling at the rock face,
toes finding purchase.
I must conquer my fear
if I want to go higher,
for I know the view
to be worth the climb.

For only in leaving behind
all that kept me bound
to the ground
can I breathe the rarified air,
and see with unimpeded clarity.

Only there will my eyes
be opened to the possibilities,
and the opportunities,
that lie in a world which will
spread out before me
like an endless carpet.

Only there can I see
what I have waited my entire life to see:
the final,
complete,
me.

I swallow my fear,
fix my gaze higher,
                    and climb.

"Every great dream begins with a dreamer. Always remember, you have within you the strength, the patience, and the passion to reach for the stars to change the world."

— Harriet Tubman

About the author:

Janet Scott McDaniel, born in Catonsville, Maryland began writing poetry at age 15, but recently emerged from a 25 year hiatus to resume her life as a poet. She has an Associate of Arts degree in fine art; and a Bachelors of Arts degree in psychology from the University of Maryland, Baltimore County.

Ms. McDaniel continues to read at open mic nights, and has had numerous poems published in online and hardcopy poetry magazines.

She was invited to read at the Legendary Women in Poetry event at Edna St. Vincent Millay's home, Steepletop, in Austerlitz, New York in July 2012.

She was also a finalist in the Fermoy, Ireland International Poetry Festival, Overseas Poetry Competition for 2012.

Ms. McDaniel currently lives on the East Coast with her husband, and her angel in black fur, Coal

THE LIGHT
and other
Collected Poems

by   Janet Scott McDaniel

The Light and other Collected Poems

Janet Scott McDaniel's first collection of poetry reflects the wide range of human emotions: love and loss, redemption and discovery, ultimate joy and the depths of introspection.

Freshly inspired, her poems weave a rich tapestry, clear and eloquent, of life in all its wonder and challenge. Photographs and background stories make this an even more intimate journey, as the voice of the poet emerges from conflict and struggle stronger than ever. Many of the pieces, while profoundly moving to any reader, are particularly empowering to women.

The book contains a selection of sixty-seven poems that strike the heart and reach into the soul, charting a unique new path into contemporary poetry.

The Light offers its readers joy, tears, and inspiration on every page.

The Light and other Collected Poems, and Parallel Dreams

Available in softcover, Kindle, and e-book:

Amazon.com
Barnesandnoble.com